CONCERT FAVORITES

Volume 2

Band Arrangements Correlated with
Essential Elements Band Method Book 1

ISBN 978-1-4234-0078-3

HAL•LEONARD®
7777 W. BLUEMOUND RD. P.O. BOX 13819 MILWAUKEE, WI 53213

BANDROOM BOOGIE

B♭ BASS CLARINET

MICHAEL SWEENEY

00860166

BEETHOVEN'S NINTH

B♭ BASS CLARINET

LUDWIG VAN BEETHOVEN
Arranged by PAUL LAVENDER

00860166

GALLANT MARCH

B♭ BASS CLARINET

MICHAEL SWEENEY

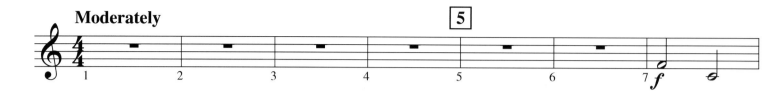

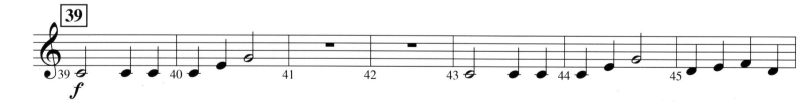

HIGH ADVENTURE

Bb BASS CLARINET

PAUL LAVENDER

00860166

ROCK & ROLL – PART II
(The Hey Song)

Bb Bass Clarinet

Words and Music by
MIKE LEANDER and GARY GLITTER
Arranged by PAUL LAVENDER

Steady Rock

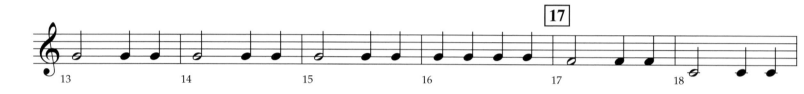

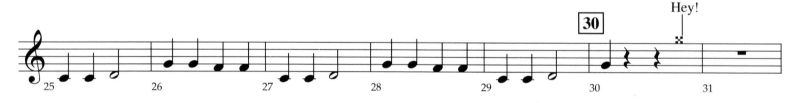

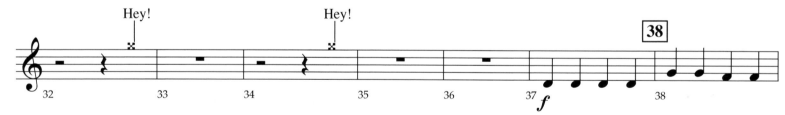

00860166

AMAZING GRACE

B♭ BASS CLARINET

Traditional American Melody
Arranged by PAUL LAVENDER

INFINITY
(Concert March)

Bb BASS CLARINET

JAMES CURNOW (ASCAP)

00860166

LATIN FIRE

B♭ BASS CLARINET

JOHN HIGGINS

00860166

LINUS AND LUCY

B♭ BASS CLARINET

By VINCE GUARALDI
Arranged by MICHAEL SWEENEY

* New Note

* New Note: A♭

00860166

THEME FROM "STAR TREK® GENERATIONS"

(From The Paramount Motion Picture STAR TREK GENERATIONS)

Bb BASS CLARINET

Music by DENNIS McCARTHY
Arranged by MICHAEL SWEENEY

00860166

AMERICAN SPIRIT MARCH

B♭ BASS CLARINET

JOHN HIGGINS

GATHERING IN THE GLEN

B♭ BASS CLARINET

MICHAEL SWEENEY

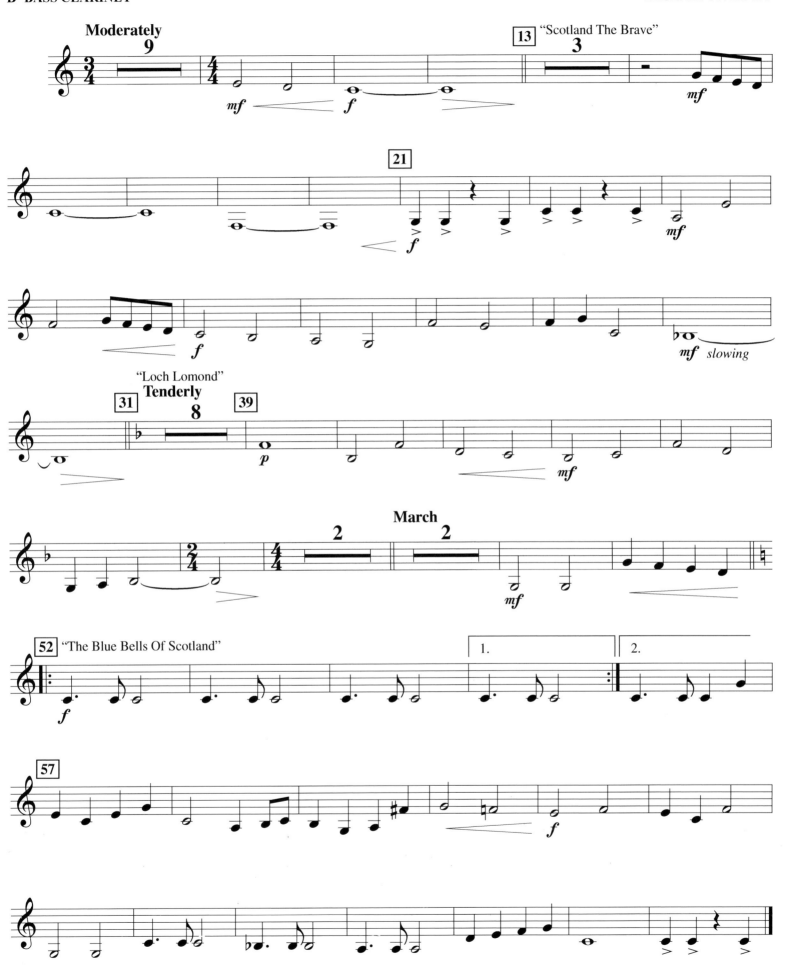

00860166

THE LOCO-MOTION

Words and Music by
GERRY GOFFIN and CAROLE KING
Arranged by JOHN HIGGINS

B♭ BASS CLARINET

Rock Style

00860166

ROYAL FIREWORKS MUSIC

GEORGE FREDERIC HANDEL
Arranged by MICHAEL SWEENEY

Bb Bass Clarinet

00860166

SCARBOROUGH FAIR

Bb Bass Clarinet

Traditional English
Arranged by JOHN MOSS